D1716706

# POLAR BEARS
## ON THE HUNT

by Jody Sullivan Rake

Reading Consultant:
Barbara J. Fox
Reading Specialist
North Carolina State University

Content Consultant:
Erich H. Follmann, PhD
Professor of Zoology
University of Alaska, Fairbanks

CAPSTONE PRESS
a capstone imprint

Blazers is published by Capstone Press,
151 Good Counsel Drive, P.O. Box 669, Mankato, Minnesota 56002.
www.capstonepress.com

092009
005619WZS10

*Library of Congress Cataloging-in-Publication Data*
Rake, Jody Sullivan.
    Polar bears : on the hunt / by Jody Sullivan Rake.
    p. cm. — (Blazers. Killer animals)
    Summary: "Describes polar bears, their habitat, hunting habits, and relationship
to people" — Provided by publisher.
    Includes bibliographical references and index.
    ISBN 978-1-4296-3927-9 (library binding)
    1. Polar bear — Juvenile literature. I. Title.
QL737.C27R35 2010
599.786 — dc22                                                2009027880

**Editorial Credits**
Mandy Robbins, editor; Kyle Grenz, designer; Svetlana Zhurkin, media researcher;
    Laura Manthe, production specialist

**Photo Credits**
Alamy/Juniors Bildarchiv, 20
Creatas, 11 (top)
Digital Vision, 11 (bottom), 14–15
Getty Images/National Geographic/Paul Nicklen, 12–13, 16–17
iStockphoto/James Richey, 26; Karel Delvoye, 22–23
Minden Pictures/Rinie Van Meurs, 6–7
Nature Picture Library/Mats Forsberg, 4–5
Peter Arnold/Biosphoto/Fred Bruemmer, 18–19; H. Schouten, 8–9; Phone Phone/
    Sylvain Cordier, 25
Photolibrary/Steven Kazlowski, 28–29
Seapics/Doc White, cover

# TABLE OF CONTENTS

Mighty White Hunter . . . . . . . . . . . . . . . . . .  4

Polar Predators . . . . . . . . . . . . . . . . . . . .  10

Ice Stalkers . . . . . . . . . . . . . . . . . . . . . .  18

Dangerous and Endangered  . . . . . . . . .  24

Diagram  . . . . . . . . . . . . . . . . . . . . . . . .  16

Glossary . . . . . . . . . . . . . . . . . . . . . . . .  30

Read More . . . . . . . . . . . . . . . . . . . . . .  31

Internet Sites . . . . . . . . . . . . . . . . . . . . .  31

Index . . . . . . . . . . . . . . . . . . . . . . . . . .  32

# MIGHTY WHITE HUNTER

A seal rests on the ice. It doesn't notice the large white bear creeping silently toward it. The whistling wind drowns out the bear's footsteps.

The huge bear charges toward the seal. In a flash, the seal is caught in the bear's teeth. The hunt is over.

# KILLER FACT

Six types of seals live in the Arctic Circle. Polar bears mainly hunt ringed and bearded seals.

Polar bears are fierce hunters. These **arctic** animals feed mainly on seals. Seal blubber is an important part of the bear's diet.

**arctic** – the frozen area around the North Pole

# POLAR PREDATORS

A polar bear's huge paws are deadly weapons. They measure 12 inches (30 centimeters) across. They are armed with 2-inch (5-centimeter) curved claws.

A polar bear has 42 jagged teeth that tear into meat and blubber. The bear's strong jaws can crush a seal's skull in one second.

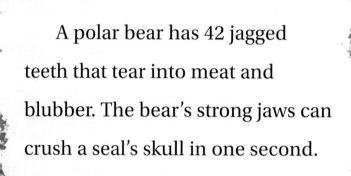

# KILLER FACT

A polar bear's teeth are larger and sharper than a grizzly bear's.

13

The bear's massive size makes it a powerful hunter. Polar bears are the heaviest land **predators**. Males can reach up to 1,500 pounds (680 kilograms).

## KILLER FACT

One of the polar bear's best weapons is its sense of smell. A polar bear can smell a seal up to 20 miles (32 kilometers) away!

**predator** – an animal that hunts other animals for food

# Polar Bear Diagram

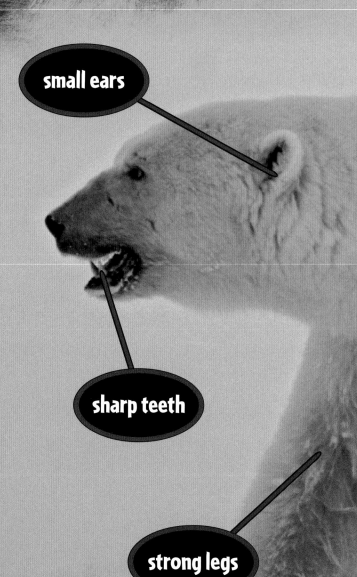

small ears

sharp teeth

strong legs

thick fur

wide paws

17

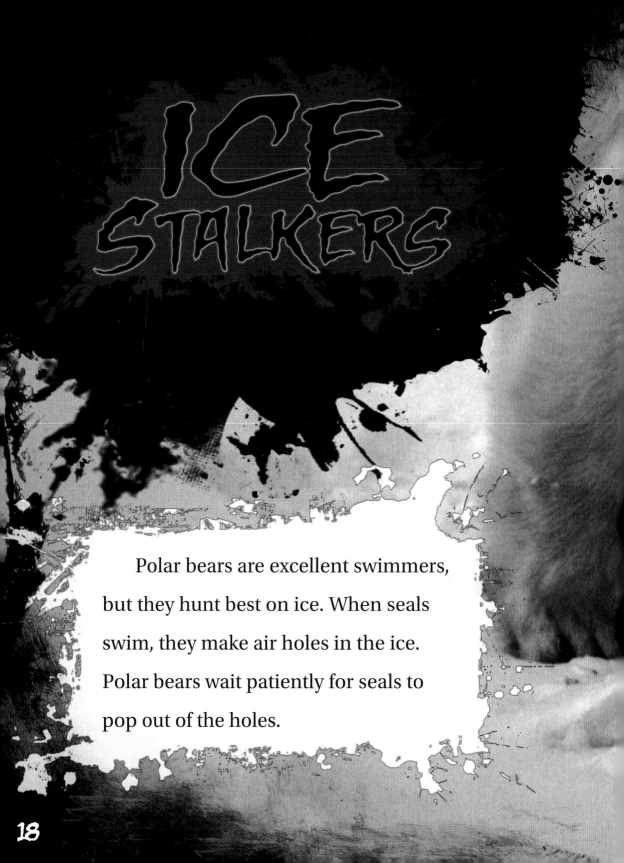

# ICE STALKERS

Polar bears are excellent swimmers, but they hunt best on ice. When seals swim, they make air holes in the ice. Polar bears wait patiently for seals to pop out of the holes.

A polar bear can smell a seal's den under the snow. The bear crashes through the snow to get its meal.

Polar bears also hunt seals that are resting on ice. Quiet, sneaky bears **stalk** seals from a distance. Then they charge. Sometimes they leap out of the water onto the seal.

**stalk** – to hunt an animal in a quiet, secret way

21

## KILLER FACT

The skin and blubber of a seal have the highest amount of fat. Hungry polar bears get energy by eating these parts first.

The polar bear bites the seal on the head to kill it. The bear drags the **prey** away from the water to eat. The polar bear eats the skin and blubber first. Then it eats the meat.

**prey** – an animal hunted by another animal for food

# DANGEROUS AND ENDANGERED

Polar bears are deadly predators. Unless polar bears are starving or teased, they will not harm people. You may never see a polar bear in the wild, but you can enjoy them in zoos.

# KILLER FACT

Churchill, in Manitoba, Canada, is called the polar bear capital of the world. Residents have spotted as many as 40 bears in town in one day.

Polar bears help balance the **ecosystem** by hunting seals. But **climate** change is shrinking the polar ice. This ice is the bear's main hunting area. Will polar bears learn to hunt on land? Only time will tell.

**ecosystem** – a group of animals and plants that work together with their surroundings

**climate** – the usual weather in a place

# Wild Bite!

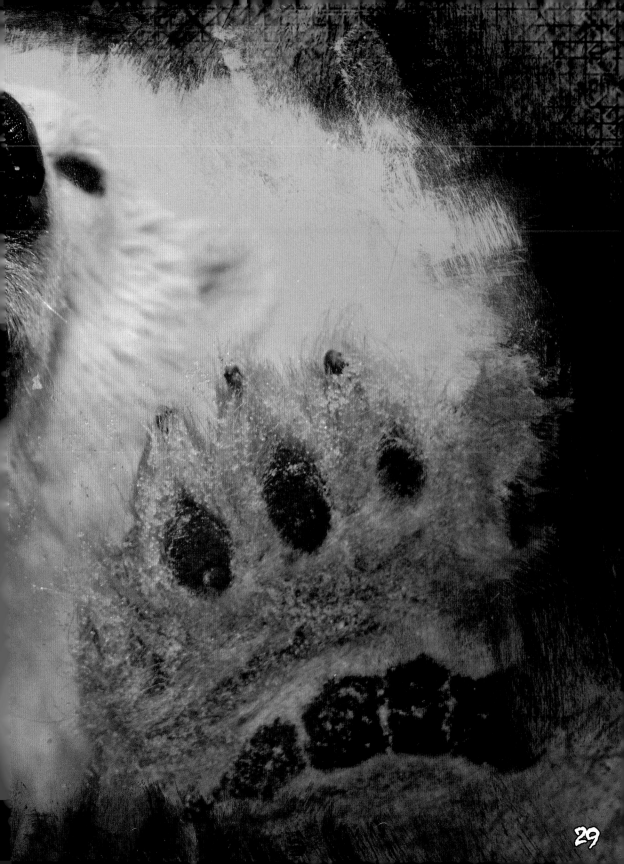

# GLOSSARY

**arctic** (ARK-tik) — the area near the North Pole

**blubber** (BLUH-buhr) — a layer of fat under the skin of some animals; blubber keeps animals warm.

**climate** (KLY-muht) — the usual weather in a place

**ecosystem** (EE-koh-sis-tuhm) — a group of animals and plants that work together with their surroundings

**predator** (PRED-uh-tur) — an animal that hunts other animals for food

**prey** (PRAY) — an animal that is hunted by another animal as food

**stalk** (STAWK) — to hunt an animal in a quiet, secret way

# READ MORE

**De Medeiros, Michael.** *Polar Bears.* Amazing Animals. New York: Weigl, 2009.

**Miller, Sara Swan.** *Polar Bears of the Arctic.* Brrr! Polar Animals. New York: PowerKids Press, 2009.

**Rosing, Norbert, and Elizabeth Carney.** *Face To Face With Polar Bears.* Face to Face. Washington, D.C.: National Geographic, 2007.

# INTERNET SITES

FactHound offers a safe, fun way to find Internet sites related to this book. All of the sites on FactHound have been researched by our staff.

Here's all you do:

Visit *www.facthound.com*

FactHound will fetch the best sites for you!

# INDEX

Arctic Circle, 9

blubber, 9, 12, 22, 23

claws, 10
climate change, 27

eating, 9, 12, 21, 22, 23
ecosystem, 27

hunting, 5, 6, 9, 15, 18,
   21, 27

jaws, 12

paws, 10
people, 24
prey. *See* seals

seals, 5, 6, 9, 12, 15, 18, 21,
   22, 23, 27
sense of smell, 5, 15, 21
size, 15
swimming, 18

teeth, 6, 12

zoos, 24